Copyright 2020 by Miroslav Nikol

This document is geared towards providing exact and reliable information in regard to the topic and issue covered. The publication is sold on the idea that the publisher is not required to render an accounting, officially permitted, or otherwise, qualified services. If advice is necessary, legal or professional, a practiced individual in the profession should be ordered.

From a Declaration of Principles which was accepted and approved equally by a Committee of the American Bar Association and a Committee of Publishers and Associations.

In no way is it legal to reproduce, duplicate, or transmit any part of this document by either electronic means or in printed format. Recording of this publication is strictly prohibited and any storage of this document is not allowed unless with written permission from the publisher. All rights reserved.

The information provided herein is stated to be truthful and consistent, in that any liability, in terms of inattention or otherwise, by any usage or abuse of any policies, processes, or Instructions: contained within is the solitary and utter responsibility of the recipient reader. Under no circumstances will any legal responsibility or blame be held against the publisher for any reparation, damages, or monetary loss due to the information herein, either directly or indirectly.

By continuing with this book, readers agree that the author is under no circumstances responsible for any losses, indirect or direct, that are incurred as a result of the information presented in this document, including, but not limited to inaccuracies, omissions and errors. Respective authors own all copyrights not held by the publisher. The information herein is offered for informational purposes solely and is universal as so.

The presentation of the information is without a contract or any type of guarantee assurance.

The information herein is offered for informational purposes solely and is universal as so. The presentation of the information is without contract or any type of guarantee assurance. Readers acknowledge that the author is not engaging in the rendering of legal, financial, medical or professional advice. Please consult a licensed professional before attempting any techniques outlined in this book.

To my dearest mother, who always cooked with love.

Table of Content

Table of Content 4

INTRODUCTION..8

Flashback 9

The food 12

Drinks and beverages 13

Diary..15

Meat...16

Seasoning 18

Fruit and Vegetables 19

Bread, pastry and desserts 20

Soups and stews 22

Secrets and specifics of Serbian cuisine................23

BREAKFAST RECIPES 28

Serbian Puttee (Uvijace)..............................29

Serbian Gruel (Kasa) 31

Sandwich (Komplet Lepinja) 33

Doughnuts (Krafne) 35

Cornbread Porridge (Kacamak) 37

Ham and Cheese Stuffed Buns (Piroske) ...39

Dried Fruits and Nut Balls 41

Cheese Pie (Burek Sa Sirom).......................43

Cheese Rolls (Kiflice) 45

APPETIZERS..47

    BBQ Shish Kebabs (Raznjici)..48

    Ajvar...50

    Kajmak...52

    Filled Eggs..54

    Appetizer Ham...56

    Piquant Mushrooms..58

    Serbian Pork Crisp (Cvarci)...60

    Gibanica with Feta Cheese..62

MAIN DISHES..64

    Stuffed Cutlet (Karadjordjeva Snicla).......................................65

    Rice with Turkey, Peppers, and Tomatoes.................................67

    Baked Sauerkraut and Turkey..69

    Ground Beef, Vegetable and Potato Bake..................................71

    Serbian Meatloaf (Veknitsa od Mesa).......................................73

    Vegetarian Sweet Cabbage (Slatki Kupus).................................75

    Potato Moussaka...77

    Serbian Chicken Fillet with Bacon..79

    Potato Pie (Pita Krompirusa)...81

    Serbian Spaghetti...83

    Pork and Peppers (Selsko Meso)...85

    Cevapcici..87

    Serbian Stuffed Cabbage (Sarma)...89

Serbian Pea Stew with Chicken 92

Potato Stuffed Peppers 94

Chicken with Peppers and Mushroom 96

Herb and Garlic Roasted Leg of Lamb 98

Filled Yellow Peppers (Punjena Paprika) 100

SOUPS AND STEWS 103

Beef Broth 104

Pork and Pepper Stew (Leskovacka Muckalica) 106

Serbian Lentils 108

Freshwater Fish Stew 110

Chicken Stew (Pileci Paprikas) 112

Cold Cucumber Soup 114

Tomato Soup 116

Cauliflower Corba 118

Lamb and Cabbage Soup (Ličani) 120

Clear Fish Soup 122

Beans Stew (Pasulj) 124

SALADS 126

Serbian Coleslaw 127

Šopska Salata 129

Oil and Vinegar Potato Salad 131

Garlic Roasted Peppers (Belolučena Paprika) 133

Cucumber Salad with Sour Cream 135

Red Beet and Carrot Salad 137

DESSERTS...139

Chocolate Balls (Čokoladne Kuglice) 140

Walnut Nutmeg Cookie..142

Serbian Fast Pastries...144

Tulumbe...146

White Bayadere (Bela Bajadera) 148

Girls' Ring (Devojački Prsten) 150

Serbian Vanilla Slice (Krempita) 152

Walnut Pie (Baklava) 154

Serbian No Bake Sand Cake...156

INTRODUCTION

The Republic of Serbia is a continental country located on the Balkan Peninsula, in south-eastern and partly in central Europe. It has a population of approximately 7 million people, with Belgrade serving as the country's capital and largest city. Serbia is a country rich in culture, traditions, diversity, and, of course, delicious cuisine -a wide range of which will be introduced to you in this book.

To truly develop a taste for a country's cuisine, one must first understand its culture, heritage, local produce, spices used, and influences from other cultures that contributed to the formation of this beautiful country. This is why it's important to start this cookbook with a quick flashback to the past.

Flashback

Members of the European ethnic group, which speak one of the Slavic languages, are known as Slavs. Serbia is one of the thirteen Slavic countries in the world. Among the others are, for example, Russia, Polan, Ukraine, Slovakia, Croatia, Slovenia and others.

Southern Slavic countries were located on the border of the Byzantine Empire in the 9th century and consequently received part of its influence, including the peculiarities of its cuisine. Serbia was a kingdom back then, which, just like any other kingdom, fought war, migrations, hunger and other political and social problems.

Serbia expanded its territory in the 12th century, encompassing what is now Albania, Montenegro, and even a portion of Greece. As a result, the cuisines of those countries have also influenced Serbian cuisine, both in terms of seasoning and with a wide variety of ingredients.

The country was further involved under the Habsburgs during the 17th century and finally gained independence in 1878 when the formal independence of the country was recognized internationally at the Congress of Berlin.

Serbia was part of Yugoslavia for much of the twentieth century. Yugoslavia literally translates to 'the land of the south Slavs' and it included the following countries: Serbia, Slovenia, Croatia, Kosovo, North Macedonia, Montenegro and Bosnia and Herzegovina. Because those countries evolved and grew together over many years, their cuisines are somewhat intertwined and similar.

However, the fall of communism and the resurgence of nationalism in the 1980s caused a schism in this union, and every country except Serbia withdrew its membership, which was followed by a major civil war that resulted in many cities being completely destroyed and thousands of deaths. One thing did not perish—the love and appetite for good food.

Nowadays, Serbian cuisine has amassed a plethora of delectable national dishes that have gained popularity not only in Serbia but also internationally. As a result of the historical background, Serbian cuisine is a fusion of indigenous Serbian flavors with elements of Middle Eastern, Mediterranean, Balkan, and Austria-Hungarian cuisine, which is precisely what makes it mouthwateringly delicious and appealing. Serbian cuisine has absorbed all of the best traditions of countries and continents with similar geographical locations, so their dishes can satisfy even the most discriminating gourmet.

The food

The Serbian government banned the use of genetically modified foods in 2009, making Serbia ineligible for membership in the World Trade Organization (WTO). This ban has since come under fire for interfering with the country's export and import sectors. Serbia is questioning the necessity of the ban and hopes to join the World Trade Organization soon.

Despite this, food products such as processed fruits and vegetables, snacks, cacao, coffee, nuts, beverage concentrates, confectionary produce, and others are imported into the country. The majority of the ingredients used in Serbian cuisine, on the other hand, are produced locally and are authentic. This makes Serbian dishes unrivaled by other cuisines around the world.

Drinks and beverages

Serbia is known for its Slivovitz, a well-known Rakia (fruit spirit) made from the Serbian national fruit, a plum, in the same way, that France is known for its cheese and wine. Fruit spirits are very popular among the locals. Rakia can have as much as 50-65 % alcohol content (ABV) if home-brewed and it is, therefore, a very heavy drink. Rakia can be made of different types of fruit: Sljivovica and Tuica are plum-based Rakias, whereas Kajsija is an apricot-based Rakia, and Lozovaca/Komovica are grape-based Rakias. Some herbs, honey, or walnuts are occasionally added to the drink.

For the Slavic people, brewing Rakia is a centuries-old tradition. Making Rakia in one's own home is a source of pride for Serbians. Rakia tasting is a ritualistic festival in Serbia that honors centuries-old traditions.

Coffee is another popular drink in Serbia. Serbians were subjected to Byzantine and Ottoman occupation in the past, which explains the prevalence of Turkish-style coffee. Coffee Arabica is the most popular type of coffee in the area. The coffee is finely ground, mixed with water, and cooked on the stovetop in a handmade copper pot before being poured into a small cup. The fine coffee grounds settle to the bottom of the cup, leaving you with a delicious cup of coffee. Usually, no milk or cream is added to the coffee, but there are small sugary desserts to go with it. Sometimes Serbians spice their day up and have some Rakia along with their morning or afternoon coffee.

Diary

Traditionally, dairy products and vegetables were the mainstays of Serbian cuisine. The meat was rarely consumed because cattle were mostly used for agriculture, and only hunted meat was consumed on rare occasions. Today, dairy products remain an important element of Serbian cuisine and are consumed on a daily basis by all people of the country, regardless of wealth.

Cow's and sheep's milk are getting increasingly popular these days. Many people, particularly in rural areas, produce their own milk, yoghurt and cheese from farm animals. Milk contributes to the exquisite flavor of hard and smoked cheeses, as well as the baking of bread and bakery products. Using milk softens them and makes them more creamy.

Kajmak is one of the most known Serbian dairy products. It is thick and fatty, made out of the skimmed milk cream. It is typically served with bread or alongside meaty foods. Serbians also produce liquid dairy products, like sour cream, sour milk (kiselo mleko) and others.

Meat

Meat is the basis of Serbian cuisine. It can be lamb, pork, or beef, and it is used to make traditional kebabs, pilaf, meatballs, and a variety of other meat meals. The majority of the people in this country prefer pork and lamb, with beef and chicken trailing in the rearview mirror. Among the most known meaty dishes are Cevapcici and Pljeskavica, which are made from different types of minced meat and seasoning, and then cooked on the grill. Grilled meat is typically served with a generous amount of fried or fresh onions and vegetables, a tasty dipping sauce, such as Ajvar, and flatbread (Lepinja). Fish and seafood are used to make soups, stews, and to fry over an open grill, but they are not as popular as meat.

Some of the other known meaty delights are:

- Karadordeva (a breaded rolled steak stuffed with sliced ham and cheese) is usually served with Tartar sauce;
- Sarma (cabbage with minced meat and rice), and other types of stuffed vegetables,
- Cvarci, homemade and organic pork fat crisps, best accompanied with something spicy.

Among the dried meat, the most common traditional dish is called Negushsky Prosciutto (dried pork). The pork is dried in the pure mountain air, and only sea salt from spices and seasonings is utilized, adding iodine to the dish. Negushsky Prosciutto is a typical appetizer that is served with homemade bread before the main dish.

Serbians often take up a traditional approach to cooking. Barbecuing is a very common method of cooking meat in Serbia, along with braising, stewing, and roasting in the oven. Restaurants sometimes used the '*pod sacem*' method or the roasting on a spit method where the meat is placed in a clay or cast-iron pot with a bell-shaped lid and covered in ash. Some dishes are especially flavorful as they are kept simmering on the stove for hours allowing the flavors to develop.

Seasoning

Serbian cuisine lacks a consistent use of spices and seasonings. In a broader sense, this is due to the Balkan peninsula's temperate climate as well as various historical influences. As a result, locals prefer to use a variety of peppers and dried herbs, such as bay leaves, dill, rosemary, thyme, or basil.

Serbians do not like to over-season their food: they prefer to achieve mouthwatering flavors with less seasoning and proper heath treatment instead.

Fruit and Vegetables

Vegetables are fairly popular among the country's citizens. Fresh, grilled, or pickled vegetables are served with every meal, on every family's table, whether for breakfast, lunch, or dinner. The vegetables grow very well in Serbia because of its warm climate. Traditionally, the vegetables are served in the form of a simple salad with olive oil or as a grilled side dish to meat. One of the locals' favorite salads is Šopska Salata, made from slices of cucumber, red and yellow paprika, tomato, onion and white cheese.

However, there are some difficult recipes in which vegetables are boiled, fried, roasted with garlic and olive oil, or pickled. Among the most popular vegetables are onions, tomatoes, potatoes, zucchini, eggplant, paprikas and cabbage.

The fruit grows well in Serbia due to the climate. It's used in a number of dishes, but it's most famous for making Rakia.

Bread, pastry and desserts

Serbian bread is known for its unique softness and airiness. Serbians often add milk to bread to make it creamier. Bread is typically served with first courses and appetizers and garnished with sesame seeds. It can be baked sweet for serving with tea or served with soups and meat. Throwing bread in the trash is thought to be a bad omen. However, this is extremely unlikely because the bread is so delicious and tender that it is devoured almost immediately.

Pies, both sweet and salty, are popular in Serbia. Tourists are perplexed because the name pie or "pita" is commonly associated with Greek bread. Pie, however, has a completely different meaning in Serbian cuisine. Lush soft pies are prepared with a variety of toppings, from nuts and fruit to cheese and meat. The variety of pies is limitless. Simultaneously, the pita varieties are cooked using the same dough recipe, regardless of whether the filling is salty or sweet – the pastry would always taste the same.

One of the most known dishes among the pita category is Burek. This dish has many varieties. The most popular Burek is made out of cheese and is very popular among the locals. Other popular fillings are spinach, minced meat and apples, as a sweet version of Burek.

Among the sweetest desserts are:

- Tulumbe, a batter that is fried and then soaked in sugar syrup.
- Tufahije, walnut stuffed apples boiled in sugar syrup with whipped cream.
- Slatko od dunja, quinces boiled in a mix of sugar, water and lemon juice and then preserved in jars.
- Vasina torta, a walnut sponge cake with creamy chocolate or walnut filling.
- Baklava, a sweet pastry pie with different types of nuts inside.

Soups and stews

Soups are a common entrée at lunch as they are considered healthy. Generally, they are called *supa* or *corba* – depending on their consistency. *Corba* is usually very thick, similar to a stew, *supa* on the other hand, is mostly clear.

Soups can be made of beef, lamb, or chicken. Sometimes, homemade noodles or are added to the soup. Stews, on the other hand, are made with a variety of ingredients, including different types of meat and vegetables. Usually, flour is used to thicken up the stews, which is unusual in many western countries.

Prebranac is by far the most known dish in this category. It is not actually considered as a stew, but it somewhat looks like it. It's a simple dish made of beans and onions, sometimes served with bacon or sausage. It requires a lot of cooking and sometimes the Serbians finish the dish in the oven so that the top layer gets crispier. It can be consumed as a main dish or as a side to grilled meat.

Among the other known stews are Mukalika (a spicy stew of pork, tomatoes and peppers), Goulash (spicy meat stew) and Podvarak (a veggie casserole).

Secrets and specifics of Serbian cuisine

Serbian cooking techniques are hardly a secret. These are rather small tricks that allow you to add a unique flavor and aroma to food.

If you try meat or fish dishes in Serbia, for example, you will most likely be surprised by their rich aroma and delicate texture. The secret to their preparation is that they are mostly cooked over an open fire with fragrant wood as fuel oil. Serbs may not season their meat with herbs and spices, preferring instead to season it with salt and pepper and allow the meat to develop its own flavor.

It is difficult to recreate such conditions at home, but you can always go outside to your yard or to a nearby park and roast or smoke your meat over a fire made out of dry cherry or walnut branches.

One of the most popular dishes in Serbia is Ajvar. It is made out of roasted peppers, eggplants and seasoning. Locals believe that true Ajvar should only be seasoned by pepper, but sophisticated chefs continue to add aromatic herbs and spices so that the dish develops a richer aroma. Every family has their own recipe for this dish, and despite using the same ingredients, the taste of Ajvar prepared by different people varies. This is because each family has its own secret, which is only passed down through inheritance.

Eating is an important part of Serbian customs and habits. It brings families and friends together; it brings neighborhoods and entire communities together. So, one of the secrets is to incorporate emotions into every plate you create. Your dishes should exude joy, friendship, and love. Emotions and a passion for cooking will elevate your dishes to a higher level.

In general, there aren't many secrets to Serbian cuisine. The main thing is to roast and smoke the meat over an open fire, add it to almost any dish as much as possible, to include flour in soups in order to thicken them, to eat seasonal salads as side dishes and to drink Turkish coffee at least twice a day. Do not forget to add some Rakija to your menu.

Being a guest in a Serbian home would be nothing less than a privilege. Be prepared to be overwhelmed by their sense of hospitality, warmth and generosity. Serbians are among the most welcoming nations and even though older generations are, in general, not great English speakers, the language barrier will dissolve after a few glasses of their home-brewed Rakia. Food is a major love language for Serbians, which they take a lot of pride in preparing. The dishes are served in massive portions and the mood around the table is always jovial.

Serbian cuisine is among the best in the world and should be tried at least once in a lifetime. So, let's dive into the world of these amazing dishes and make all of these ourselves rather than just reading about them. Shall we?

RECIPE

BOOK

BREAKFAST RECIPES

Serbian Puttee (Uvijace)

| Prep time: 5 min | Cook time: 20 min | Servings: 4 |

Ingredients

- *4 tbsp oil*
- *2 eggs*
- *Salt to taste*
- *4 tbsp flour*
- *2 cups hot water*
- *8 bread slices, not fresh*
- *Sugar for garnish*

Instructions

- Pour ½ tbsp of oil into a pan and heat it over medium heat.
- In a bowl mix the egg, salt, flour, and water.

- Immerse a bread slice in the egg mixture and place it in the heated oil.
- Bake the bread slice for 2 minutes on each side.
- Repeat the process for all the bread slices.
- Sparkle with some sugar and serve.

Nutrition-Per Serving: Calories: 320Kcal, Total Fat: 20g, Total Carbs: 26g, Protein: 7g

Tips: Do you have some leftover bread slices in your kitchen? This Serbian puttee utilizes each slice of bread and serves you a delicious breakfast. It's perfect when served with a cup of hot coffee.

Serbian Gruel (Kasa)

| Prep time: 5 min | Cook time: 25 min | Servings: 4 |

Ingredients

- *1 cup wheat flour*
- *7 tbsp water*
- *¼ cup cream cheese*
- *1 cup milk*
- *¼ cup feta cheese*

Instructions

- In a skillet mix wheat flour with water.
- Stir in cream cheese and milk into the wheat flour mixture.
- Cook the gruel over medium heat while constantly stirring until it gets smooth and compact. Cook for 20 minutes.

- Add cheddar to the gruel and cook for an additional 5 minutes.
- Serve while warm.

Nutrition-Per Serving: Calories: 217Kcal, Total Fat: 8g, Total Carbs: 29g, Protein: 8g

Tips: Kick off your day with this simple yet nutritious meal that is prepared in less than 30 minutes. It is highly packed with fiber and thus keeps you full until the next meal.

Sandwich (Komplet Lepinja)

| Prep time: 30 min | Cook time: 25 min | Servings: 2 |

Ingredients

- ¼ tbsp sugar
- 1 ¼ tbsp fresh yeast
- 1 ¼ cup warm water
- 1 cup flour
- ½ tbsp salt
- 2 tbsp olive oil
- 2 eggs, beaten
- 6 tbsp roasting meat juice
- 1 ¾ oz prosciutto, sliced

Instructions

- In a bowl add the sugar, yeast, and water. Allow the yeast to foam.
- Add flour, salt, and oil to the yeast mixture and knead into a smooth dough. Let the dough stand for 20 minutes.
- Form 2 balls from the dough and allow it to stand for 10 minutes.
- Preheat the oven to 390°F.
- Form buns from the dough and place them in a baking tray.
- Bake the buns for 15 minutes.
- Remove the buns from the oven and allow them to cool for 5 minutes. Cut the buns into halves.
- Crack an egg over two buns and bake for 2 minutes.
- Build the sandwich by pouring roasting meat juices over the baked bun and top with prosciutto.
- Place the remaining buns over the prosciutto.
- Serve while warm.

Nutrition-Per Serving: Calories: 532Kcal, Total Fat: 25g, Total Carbs: 53g, Protein: 22g

Tips: This unique sandwich is made of a crunchy bun and has a buttery inside. Serbians would made it out of Negushsky Prosciutto and would eat it also as an appetizer prior to main dish.

Doughnuts (Krafne)

Prep time: 2 h Cook time: 20 min Servings: 36 pieces

Ingredients

- *1 cup milk*
- *4 oz butter*
- *¼ cup sugar*
- *2 tbsp salt*
- *2 ¼ tbsp active dry yeast*
- *1 cup hot water*
- *3 eggs, beaten*
- *6 cups all-purpose flour*
- *4 cups cooking oil*
- *Confectioners' sugar for garnish*

Instructions

- Pour milk into a saucepan and scald it.
- Add butter, sugar, and salt to the milk then stir until all the butter is completely dissolved.
- In a bowl dissolve the yeast in hot water.
- Stir the milk mixture and eggs into the yeast mixture.
- Stir the flour gradually into the milk mixture until a smooth dough is formed.
- Cover the dough and let it stand for 1 hour.
- Roll out the dough on a floured flat surface into ½-inch thickness.
- Using a cookie cutter cut the dough into 3-inch circles.
- Cover the doughnuts and allow them to stand for 30 minutes.
- Heat oil in a deep frying pan over medium heat and place the donuts in a deep-frying basket.
- Deep fry the doughnuts for about 15 minutes until they are light brown on both sides.
- Place the doughnut on a shallow dish lined with a paper towel to absorb excess grease.
- Roll the doughnuts in confectioners' sugar and serve.

Nutrition-Per Serving: Calories: 271Kcal, Total Fat: 28g, Total Carbs: 4g, Protein: 1g

Tips: These delicious treats are among the tastiest baked goods from a donut shop when served hot. The good news is you can prepare them for your family on any morning.

Cornbread Porridge (Kacamak)

| Prep time: 5 min | Cook time: 10 min | Servings: 2 |

Ingredients

- 2 cups water
- 2 tbsp butter
- ½ tbsp salt
- 1 cup yellow cornmeal

Instructions

- Add water, butter, and salt to a saucepan and bring the mixture to a boil over medium heat.
- Reduce the heat to low and add cornmeal to the boiling water.
- Stir the mixture until the cornmeal is well incorporated.

- Cook the porridge for about 2 minutes until it thickens.
- Plate the porridge and garnish with feta cheese.
- Serve and enjoy.

Nutrition-Per Serving: Calories: 407Kcal, Total Fat: 14g, Total Carbs: 63g, Protein: 7g

Tips: This is a hearty meal to start off your day with. It is filling and energizing hence perfect when you have some physical activities to perform during the morning hours.

Ham and Cheese Stuffed Buns (Piroske)

| Prep time: 6 h 30 min | Cook time: 15 min | Servings: 12 pieces |

Ingredients

- 4 ½ cups all-purpose flour
- 1 ½ lb. crumbled feta cheese
- 4 eggs, beaten
- 2 tbsp olive oil
- 2 tbsp granulated sugar
- 5 tbsp baking powder
- 1 cup canola oil

For the filling

- 12 slices ham
- 12 mozzarella sticks

Instructions

- Add all the dough ingredients to a food processor.

- Mix the mixture until a soft dough forms.
- Place the dough in a bowl and knead it into a ball.
- Transfer the dough to an oiled bowl and refrigerate it for at least 4 hours.
- Wrap each mozzarella stick with a slice of ham.
- Roll out the dough on a floured surface to ¼ -inch thickness.
- Cut the dough into 12 rectangles.
- Place the wrapped cheese on the rectangles and roll them up to seal.
- Roll the sealed dough over a floured surface and place them in a shallow dish.
- Cover the Piroske with a towel and refrigerate for 2 hours.
- Heat oil in a skillet over medium heat and deep fry the Piroske in batches for 6 minutes. Turn them gently to ensure they brown evenly.
- Serve with ketchup and mayo or pickles.

Nutrition-Per Serving: Calories: 601Kcal, Total Fat: 37g, Total Carbs: 41g, Protein: 26g

Tips: These cheese stuffed buns are very tasty and easy to put together. They have a melted cheesy perfection on the inside that leaves you craving for more.

Dried Fruits and Nut Balls

| Prep time: 10 min | Cook time: 45 min | Servings: 4 |

Ingredients

- 3 oz almonds
- 8 oz dried and diced fruits (prunes, dates, strawberries, cranberries, currants, apricot, fig, and raisins)
- 2 ½ oz ground cookies
- 3 oz piloncillo sugar
- 1 tbsp lemon juice
- 3 oz unsalted butter

Instructions

- Preheat the oven to 350°F.
- Place the almonds on a baking sheet and roast them for 15 minutes. Allow them to cool.
- Add the almonds to a food processor and grind them.

- In a bowl mix the dried fruits, almonds, and ground cookies.
- Add the sugar, lemon juice, and butter to a skillet and mix.
- Heat the sugar mixture for about 30 minutes over medium heat until all the sugar melts.
- Stir the almond mixture into the sugar mixture.
- Make balls from the almond mixture and place them on a serving platter.
- Stick a lollipop stick on each ball.
- Serve and enjoy.

Nutrition-Per Serving: Calories: 485Kcal, Total Fat: 46g, Total Carbs: 17g, Protein: 7g

Tips: Kick up your energies with these nut balls. They are easy to prepare yet very delicious and packed with nutrients.

Cheese Pie (Burek Sa Sirom)

| Prep time: 30 min | Cook time: 30 min | Servings: 6 |

Ingredients

- 1 lb. crumbled goat cheese
- 8 oz softened cream cheese (or sour cream)
- 2 beaten eggs
- 4 tbsp freshly chopped parsley
- 2 tbsp freshly chopped dill
- Package filo dough
- ½ cup melted butter
- ½ cup olive oil

Directions

- In a bowl mix the goat cheese and cream cheese until they get fluffy.

- Stir in the eggs, parsley, and dill to the cheese until well combined.
- Separate the dough into two piles of each 24 sheets
- Cut the dough into halves then cover it with a paper towel.
- Preheat the oven to 375°F.
- In a separate bowl mix the butter and olive and brush a pan with the mixture.
- Place 2 filo sheets on a flat surface and brush them with the butter mixture.
- Place the 2 more sheets over the others.
- Spread ⅙ of the cheese mixture over the filo sheets.
- Lay 2 filo sheets over the cheese mixture and brush them with the butter mixture.
- Place another 2 filo sheets over the pie and tuck the edges to form a round-shaped pie.
- Repeat the process for the remaining pies.
- Transfer the pie to the greased pan and bake them for about 30 minutes until they turn golden brown.
- Serve and enjoy.

Nutrition - per serving: Calories: 915 kcal, Total fat: 71g, Carbs: 46g, Protein: 24g

Tips: You can substitute the cheese filling with minced meat or spinach. Locals usually consume Burek along with some plain white yoghurt.

Cheese Rolls (Kiflice)

| Prep time: 1h 45 min | Cook time: 20 min | Servings: 20 pieces |

Ingredients

- *1 cup feta cheese*
- *1 egg white*
- *1 cup milk*
- *2 tbsp active dry yeast*
- *1 tbsp sugar*
- *2 cups all-purpose flour*
- *1 tbsp salt*
- *1 egg, beaten*
- *¼ cup sunflower oil*
- *1 egg yolk*
- *1 tbsp milk*

- *1 tbsp sesame seeds*
- *½ cup margarine, cut int0 pieces*

Instructions

- In a bowl add cheese and egg white and crush the cheese using a fork. Set aside.
- Warm ½ cup of milk and add yeast, sugar, and 1 tbsp flour.
- Let the yeast mixture stand for 30 minutes.
- In a bowl, sift flour and salt. Add the yeast mixture, egg, oil, and the remaining ½ cup of milk to the flour mixture and mix until smooth dough is formed.
- Cover the dough and let it stand for 1 hour.
- Knead the dough and divide it into 5 balls. Roll out a dough ball using a rolling pin and cut it into 4 triangles.
- Place a spoonful of cheese mixture at the base of the triangle and fold the edges. Roll the dough to seal.
- Repeat the process for all the dough balls.
- In a bowl mix the egg yolk with 1 tablespoon of milk.
- Brush the dough rolls with the egg mixture and sprinkle with sesame seeds.
- Preheat the oven to 350°F and place the dough rolls on a baking sheet. Arrange the margarine pieces between the rolls.
- Bake the cheese rolls for 20 minutes, then serve and enjoy!

Nutrition-Per Serving: Calories: 93Kcal, Total Fat: 4g, Total Carbs: 10g, Protein: 2g

Tips: These fluffy rolls are perfect for a classic breakfast. The savory flavor of cheese makes them addictive. They are a great accompaniment to your morning cup of coffee.

APPETIZERS

BBQ Shish Kebabs (Raznjici)

| Prep time: 20 min | Cook time: 20 min | Servings: 6 |

Ingredients

- *2 lb. pork, boneless*
- *Salt and black pepper*
- *2 tbsp vegetable oil*
- *2 garlic cloves, minced*
- *1 cup onions, sliced plus ½ finely minced*
- *15 small bay leaves*

Instructions

- Pat the pork cubes dry with a paper towel.
- Sprinkle the dried meat with salt and pepper to taste.
- Place the pork in a microwave-safe bowl then add oil, garlic and sliced onions.

- Let marinate in the fridge for at least 3 hours while stirring occasionally.
- Meanwhile, soak skewers in water for 30minutes.
- Heat your broiler. Thread the 7 pork cubes on the skewer alternating with the bay leaves and discard the marinade.
- Broil for 10 minutes or until the internal temperature is 16F
- Sprinkle with minced onions and serve.

Nutrition- Per Serving: Calories 444kcal, Total Fat: 25g, Carbs: 10g, Protein: 43g

Tips: These are among the best tasting kebabs you can easily make in your home. You may use pork meat solely or alternate with some lamb or veal. Sometimes, a few pieces of vegetables, such as onions or paprikas, are threaded between the meat pieces as well.

Ajvar

Prep time: 20 min　　Cook time: 3 hours　　Servings: 8

Ingredients

- 1 lb. eggplant
- 4 lb. red peppers
- 2 garlic cloves
- 1 ¼ cup vegetable oil
- 3 tbsp vinegar
- 2 tbsp salt

Instructions

- Poke holes on the eggplant and peppers then roast them separately in the oven for 40 minutes or until soft.
- Place them in a separate bowl covered with plastic wrap. Let rest for 1 hour to cool.
- Remove the peels and seeds of the peppers then wash them well with clean water. Remove the eggplant peels.
- Add the peppers, eggplants, and garlic cloves in a food processor and pulse until finely chopped.
- Heat oil in a pot and add the pureed mixture. Stir well with a wooden spoon and add vinegar and salt.
- Cook while occasionally stirring for 2 hours over low heat. Consume the Ajvar within a week, can it or store in a fridge.

Nutrition- Per Serving: Calories: 408kcal, Total Fat: 35g, Carbs: 24g, Protein: 5g

Tips: Ajvar is a spread that is popular throughout Bosnia, Croatia and Serbia. It's tangy, rich in flavors, yet very easy to put together. It can be served as an appetizer as well as a condiment. Usually, people eat it along some grilled meat and Lepinja.

Kajmak

| Prep time: 5 min | Cook time: 5 hours | Servings: 12 |

Ingredients

- *8 cups raw cow milk*
- *1 tbsp salt*

Instructions

- Pour the milk into a saucepan and bring it to a boil.
- Allow the milk to cool completely without stirring.
- Skim off the cream at the top and put it in a bowl.

- Repeat the boiling, cooling, and skimming off process to get plenty of the cream.
- Add salt to the cream and mix well.
- Serve with bread or as a side to grilled meat.

Nutrition - per serving: Calories: 595kcal, Total fat: 32g, Carbs: 47g, Protein: 31g

Tips: This is a homemade spread for bread slices and hamburger patties which is extracted from unhomogenized milk. This sweet cream has a fluffy texture that cheese lovers can't resist. It is served as a side dish next to meat and bread at every picking or family gathering.

Filled Eggs

| Prep time: 10 min | Cook time: 10 min | Servings: 6 |

Ingredients

- *6 eggs*
- *½ stick butter*
- *3 tbsp mustard*
- *½ tbsp parsley*
- *Salt and pepper to taste*

Instructions

- Add water and eggs in a saucepan such that the eggs are submerged.

- Boil the eggs for 10 minutes. Transfer the eggs to ice cold water and peel them.
- Cut the eggs into halves, remove the yolk and place it in a mixing bowl.
- Add butter, mustard, parsley, salt and pepper. Mix until well combined.
- Fill the egg white halves with the mixture. Sprinkle with more parsley and green onion.
- Serve and enjoy!

Nutrition- Per Serving: Calories 157kcal, Total Fat: 14g, Carbs: 3g, Protein: 8g

Tips: This is an excellent appetizer to serve your family. It's easy to make yet so tasty that you will want to make it over and over again.

Appetizer Ham

| Prep time: 15 min | Cook time: 35 min | Servings: 4 |

Ingredients

- *3 lb. spinach*
- *⅓ cup flour*
- *½ stick butter*
- *5 oz milk*
- *Salt and pepper to taste*
- *5 oz cheese*
- *2 eggs, cooked and shredded*
- *4 flaps ham*
- *1 tbsp curry*

Instructions

- Wash spinach and cook them in salted water for 15 minutes
- Meanwhile, fry flour in butter for 2 minutes. Add milk and mix well until it gets thick,
- Add salt, pepper, and ⅔ of the cheese.
- Mix the shredded eggs in 6 tbsp of the sauce and 6 tbsp of the spinach cooking water. Add the remaining cheese.
- Coat the hams with the mixture and fold them into rolls.
- Coarsely cut the cooked spinach and place them in a baking dish.
- Place the ham rolls at the top and bake in the oven for 10 minutes

Nutrition- Per Serving: Calories 445kcal, Total Fat: 29g, Carbs: 24g, Protein: 30g

Tips: This is an excellent way to use leftover ham. The appetizer comes out so delicious that one roll can never be enough.

Piquant Mushrooms

| Prep time: 10 min | Cook time: 20 min | Servings: 3 |

Ingredients

- 2 tbsp oil
- ½ lb. mushrooms
- 2 flaps garlic
- Piece bay leaf
- Salt and pepper
- 2 garlic cloves
- ½ cup wine
- 1 lemon juice
- 2 eggs, sliced into quarters

Instructions

- Clean the mushrooms and cut them into thin slices.
- Heat oil on a saucepan and sauté mushrooms, garlic, bay leaf, pepper, and garlic cloves.
- Add salt and wine and cook for additional minutes.
- Add lemon and cook for 15 minutes. Transfer to a container and let rest to chill.
- Add eggs to the mushrooms, stir well and serve immediately.

Nutrition- Per Serving: Calories 174kcal, Total Fat: 12g, Carbs: 5g, Protein: 6g

Tips: This simple appetizer dish takes your mushrooms to the next level. The combination of the mushrooms and boiled eggs makes it even better and a perfect crowd pleaser dish to serve during gatherings. Serve with sauce of your choice.

Serbian Pork Crisp (Cvarci)

| Prep time: 10 min | Cook time: 30 min | Servings: 8 |

Ingredients

- *2 ¾ lb. bacon, cut into small cubes*
- *1 onion, chopped*

Instructions

- Fry bacon on a pan for 20 minutes until it melts.
- Stir in the onions to the bacon and fry for 6 minutes.
- Drain the liquid fat and discard.
- You can eat them as a snack or use them as a garnish for pasta, potatoes, salad and other dishes!

Nutrition-Per Serving: Calories: 745Kcal, Total Fat: 73g, Total Carbs: 1g, Protein: 19g

Tips: These mouthwatering sweet pork crisps serve you an appetizer of the year. It requires just two ingredients to make but tastes like heaven. Just like grownups, kids love them as well.

Gibanica with Feta Cheese

| Prep time: 30 min | Cook time: 60 min | Servings: 7 |

Ingredients

- 8 oz cream cheese
- 9 eggs
- ½ lb. feta cheese
- 2 ½ lb. cottage cheese
- 1 lb. filo dough
- 8 oz butter, melted

Instructions

- Beat cream cheese in a mixing bowl until fluffy.
- Add 3 eggs at a time beating the mixture after every addition.

- Add feta and cottage cheese then mix well.
- Preheat your oven to 350F.
- Fold two filo dough sheets and place them in a buttered baking pan.
- Brush the filo dough with butter then spread half a cup of the filling. Repeat the process until the sheets of the dough are left.
- Top everything with the three sheets of filo dough and brush with the remaining butter.
- Place the pan on a rimmed baking sheet and bake for an hour.
- Let rest for 20 minutes before cutting into squares and serving.

Nutrition- Per Serving: Calories: 729kcal, Total Fat: 51g, Carbs: 38g, Protein: 30g

Tips: This Serbian Gibanica is one great example of Serbian pie. The good news is that you may omit the type of cheese you dislike and replace it with your favorite or even fill it with some other ingredients, such as minced meat or veggies if desired.

MAIN DISHES

Stuffed Cutlet (Karadjordjeva Snicla)

| Prep time: 10 min | Cook time: 10 min | Servings: 4 |

Ingredients

- 4 pork cutlets
- 4 oz cream cheese
- Salt and black pepper to taste
- 8 slices smoked ham
- 8 pieces mozzarella string cheese
- 2 eggs, beaten
- 2 cups all-purpose flour
- 3 cups breadcrumbs
- Oil for frying
- Lettuce leaves
- Ketchup

Instructions

- Place each cutlet on a flat surface and pound them into ¼-inch thickness using a meat mallet.
- Spread cream cheese on the cutlets and sprinkle them with salt and pepper.
- Place 2 slices of ham over the cream cheese and mozzarella piece at the center of the cutlet.
- Roll up the cutlets and secure them with toothpicks.
- Place the eggs, flour, and breadcrumbs in different bowls.
- Coat the cutlet rolls with flour, dip them in the eggs, and finally coat them with breadcrumbs. Shake off excess breadcrumbs and repeat the coating process for the cutlets.
- Heat oil in a skillet over medium heat and place the schnitzels in a deep-frying basket with the seam side down.
- Deep fry the schnitzels for about 10 minutes until they turn golden brown.
- Transfer the schnitzels to a shallow dish lined with a paper towel to absorb excess grease.
- Serve the schnitzels with lettuce leaves and ketchup.

Nutrition-Per Serving: Calories: 949Kcal, Total Fat: 62g, Total Carbs: 50g, Protein: 41g

Tips: Impress your guests with this delicious and finger-licking dish. It has different flavors all rolled into one schnitzel. The dish comes together in less than 30 minutes.

Rice with Turkey, Peppers, and Tomatoes

| Prep time: 15 min | Cook time: 20 min | Servings: 4 |

Ingredients

- 2 tbsp canola oil
- 1 lb. turkey breast cut into small cubes
- Salt and black pepper to taste
- 2 onions, chopped
- 2 garlic cloves, chopped
- 2 red peppers, diced
- 2 green peppers, diced
- 1 tbsp sweet paprika
- 1 tbsp hot paprika
- 7 oz long-grain rice, cleaned and rinsed
- 2 tbsp tomato paste

- *2 ½ cups chicken broth*
- *14 oz diced tomatoes*
- *Parsley, chopped*

Instructions

- Heat oil in a skillet over medium heat and brown the turkey for 2 minutes.
- Season the turkey with salt and pepper.
- Stir in onions, garlic, and bell peppers to the turkey and cook for 1 minute.
- Add paprika to the turkey and stir to mix. Stir rice and tomato paste into the turkey.
- Stir the broth and diced tomatoes into the rice mixture and bring it to a boil.
- Cook the rice while covered for 20 minutes while stirring often.
- Serve while hot.

Nutrition-Per Serving: Calories: 399Kcal, Total Fat: 7g, Total Carbs: 47g, Protein: 36g

Tips: This rice is packed with dietary fiber and protein that are essential in boosting your health. It is also very easy to prepare and satisfying.

Baked Sauerkraut and Turkey

| Prep time: 15 min | Cook time: 1 h | Servings: 8 |

Ingredients

- 2 tbsp pork oil
- 1 chopped yellow onion
- 5 oz bacon pieces
- 1 minced garlic clove
- 1 carrot, sliced
- 32 oz sauerkraut, drained
- 2 bay leaves
- Black pepper to taste
- 1 tbsp sweet paprika
- 1 lb. smoked turkey
- ½ cup water
- 8 red pepper

Instructions

- Preheat the oven to 375°F.
- Heat pork oil in a skillet over medium heat and sauté onions and bacon for 5 minutes.
- Stir in garlic, carrots, sauerkraut, bay leaves, pepper, and paprika to the bacon.
- Cook the sauerkraut for 10 minutes while stirring occasionally.
- Transfer the sauerkraut mixture to a baking dish and top it with smoked turkey.
- Add water to the sauerkraut and bake covered for 45 minutes.
- Discard the bay leaves and serve with red pepper.

Nutrition-Per Serving: Calories: 264Kcal, Total Fat: 22g, Total Carbs: 2g, Protein: 12g

Tips: This is a simple, nourishing, and delicious meal that is a perfect choice for a busy weeknight dinner. Sauerkraut is often used in Serbian cuisine. Usually, locals make their version at home.

Ground Beef, Vegetable and Potato Bake

| Prep time: 25 min | Cook time: 1 h | Servings: 4 |

Ingredients

- 1 lb. ground beef
- 1 tbsp olive oil
- 1 chopped green pepper
- 1 chopped onion
- 1 shredded carrot
- 2 chopped celery stalks
- ½ tbsp paprika
- ½ tbsp salt
- ¾ tbsp black pepper
- ¼ tbsp crushed red pepper
- 1 pinch ground cinnamon

- *1 pinch ground garlic clove*
- *¼ cup water*
- *⅛ cup red wine*
- *1 cube beef bouillon*
- *2 tbsp half and half*
- *2 peeled potatoes, sliced*
- *Basil*

Instructions

- Preheat the oven to 400°F. In a skillet brown the beef for 5 minutes.
- Remove the beef from the skillet and set it aside. Reserve the cooking juices.
- Pour oil into the skillet and sauté green pepper, onion, carrot, and celery for 3 minutes.
- Stir in beef, paprika, salt, black pepper, red pepper, cinnamon, and garlic cloves, water, and red wine to the skillet.
- Dissolve the bouillon cube in the beef mixture.
- Remove the beef mixture from heat and stir in half and half.
- Layer some potato slices at the bottom of a baking dish.
- Transfer the beef mixture into the baking dish and top with the remaining potatoes. Cook covered for 45 minutes.

Nutrition-Per Serving: Calories: 367Kcal, Total Fat: 18g, Total Carbs: 27g, Protein: 23g

Tips: Prepare this dish on a cold day for lunch or dinner. It is highly satisfying and will keep hunger at bay for hours. It's also a great way to use some leftover meat or potatoes – do not hesitate to add different types of meat, such as pork or lamb, to the dish.

Serbian Meatloaf (Veknitsa od Mesa)

| Prep time: 15 min | Cook time: 1 h 50 min | Servings: 4 |

Ingredients

- 2 tbsp olive oil
- 8 smoked, streaky, rindless bacon slices
- 2 lean bacon slices, diced
- 1 finely chopped onion
- 1 garlic clove, crushed
- ½ cup breadcrumbs
- ¼ cups milk
- 15 oz lean minced beef
- 15 oz lean minced pork
- ½ tbsp freshly chopped thyme

- *2 tbsp freshly chopped parsley*
- *2 eggs, beaten*
- *Parsley for garnishing*

Instructions

- Preheat the oven to 400°F and brush a meatloaf tin with oil.
- Layer the streaky bacon slices on the loaf tin.
- Fry the diced bacon in a frying pan for about 5 minutes until it gets crispy.
- Stir in onion and garlic to the bacon and cook for 3 minutes.
- Soak the breadcrumbs in milk for 5 minutes.
- Stir in minced meats, bacon, onion mixture, thyme, parsley, and eggs to the breadcrumbs.
- Spoon the meat mixture into the loaf pan and level with a spoon.
- Bake the meatloaf for 1 ½ hour.
- Slice and garnish with parsley.
- Serve and enjoy.

Nutrition-Per Serving: Calories: 485Kcal, Total Fat: 46g, Total Carbs: 17g, Protein: 7g

Tips: Ever tried a meatloaf? If not, this is a must try recipe. It comes out tender and juicy on the inside while the edges are crispy. The loaf also has an irresistible flavor. Serve it next to some mashed potatoes or steamed veggies.

Vegetarian Sweet Cabbage (Slatki Kupus)

| Prep time: 10 min | Cook time: 5 min | Servings: 6 |

Ingredients

- *⅛ cup olive oil*
- *2 white onions, chopped*
- *2 cups water*
- *1 carrot, grated*
- *1 cabbage head, chopped into small pieces*
- *1 bay leaf*
- *salt to taste*
- *1 tbsp minced red peppers*
- *ground black pepper to taste*
- *1 tomato, diced*
- *2 garlic cloves, minced*
- *2 tbsp parsley*

- *parsley for garnishing*

Instructions

- Heat oil and onions in a saucepan over medium heat.
- Add 2 tbsp of water to the onion and allow it to steam for about 3 minutes.
- Stir in carrots to the onions and cook for 5 minutes.
- Stir in the cabbage, bay leaf, salt, and remaining water to the carrot mixture. Simmer for 10 minutes.
- Add red peppers and ground peppers to the cabbage and mix. Cook for 3 minutes.
- Stir tomato, garlic, and parsley into the cabbage and allow simmering for 15 minutes.
- Garnish with parsley and serve.

Nutrition-Per Serving: Calories: 99Kcal, Total Fat: 5g, Total Carbs: 13g, Protein: 2g

Tips: Sweet cabbage is a frugal way to incorporate veggies in your family meals. It is delicious and can be served on its own or with rice or bread

Potato Moussaka

Prep time: 30 min   Cook time: 1h 15 min   Servings: 2

Ingredients

- ¼ cup olive oil
- 1 chopped onion
- 1 lb. ground beef
- Salt and black pepper to taste
- 4 lb. russet potatoes, peeled and sliced

For the Topping:

- 4 eggs, beaten
- 1 cup sour cream
- 2 cups milk
- Salt and black pepper to taste

Instructions

- Heat oil in a skillet over medium heat and sauté the onions for 3 minutes.
- Stir in the meat and season it with salt and pepper.
- Using a fork break up the meat until it is browned.
- Preheat the oven to 400°F and brush a baking dish with oil.
- Lay half of the potatoes on the baking dish and season them with salt and pepper.
- Spread the meat over the potatoes and layer the remaining potatoes on top.
- In a bowl whisk the eggs, sour cream, milk, salt, and pepper.
- Pour the egg mixture over the potatoes.
- Bake the potatoes for 1 hour.
- Allow the Mousaka to stand for 10 minutes before slicing.
- Serve and enjoy.

Nutrition - per serving: Calories: 2045kcal, Total fat:92g, Carbs: 195g, Protein: 111g

Tips: This a wonderful and delicious dish to serve for a light lunch or dinner. It uses ingredients readily available in your pantry, but the end results are irresistible.

Serbian Chicken Fillet with Bacon

| Prep time: 20 min | Cook time: 40 min | Servings: 4 |

Ingredients

- *7 oz chicken thighs, boneless, cut into small pieces*
- *Salt and black pepper to taste*
- *4 bacon slices*
- *Thyme sprigs*

Instructions

- Add the chicken, salt, and pepper to a bowl and mix.
- Leave the chicken to marinate for 10 minutes.
- Place the bacon slices on a flat surface and divide the chicken pieces among the bacon slices.
- Wrap the chicken with the bacon and secure with a toothpick.

- Place the bacon-wrapped chicken on a baking sheet and bake in a preheated oven at 390°F for 40 minutes.
- Remove the toothpicks from the bacon-wrapped chicken.
- Garnish with thyme sprigs and serve.

Nutrition-Per Serving: Calories: 224Kcal, Total Fat: 19g, Total Carbs: 2g, Protein: 12g

Tips: Let's face it! Who doesn't love bacon? This bacon-wrapped chicken serves a scrumptious dish that you and your family will fall in love with. It is crispy on the outside and juicy on the inside.

Potato Pie (Pita Krompirusa)

Prep time: 55 min   Cook time: 1 h   Servings: 10

Ingredients

- 2 cups wheat flour
- Salt to taste
- 1 tbsp rapeseed oil
- 1 ¼ cup lukewarm water
- 1 tbsp Vegeta seasoning
- ¼ cup boiling water
- 1 tbsp sesame seeds

For the filling

- 2 tbsp rapeseed oil
- 1 onion, diced
- ½ lb. plant-based mince

- *2 lb. potatoes, peeled and cut into cubes*
- *2 tbsp Vegeta seasoning*
- *Black pepper to taste*

Instructions

- In a bowl add flour, a pinch of salt, oil, and lukewarm water then mix until a smooth dough is formed. Set aside.
- Prepare the filling by heating oil in a skillet and sauté the onions for 2 minutes. Add the vegan mince to the skillet and mix.
- Stir the potatoes into the skillet and cook the potatoes for 10 minutes.
- Season the potatoes with 2 tablespoon Vegeta pepper then cool them for 30 minutes. Preheat the oven to 400° F.
- Knead the dough and divide it into 2 parts.
- Flour a flat surface and roll out the dough until it gets thin.
- Place half of the potato mixture on the rolled-out dough and roll to seal. Repeat the process with the remaining dough.
- Place the rolled dough on a baking sheet and bake for 35 minutes.
- In a bowl mix 1 tablespoon Vegeta seasoning and boiling water.
- Brush the dough rolls with the seasoning mixture and sprinkle them with sesame seeds.
- Bake the dough rolls for an additional 25 minutes. Serve warm.

Nutrition-Per Serving: Calories: 316Kcal, Total Fat: 7g, Total Carbs: 50g, Protein: 11g

Tips: This potato pie is baked to perfection in your oven. It creates a divine aroma while cooking that makes everyone want to eat it.

Serbian Spaghetti

Prep time: 15 min   Cook time: 20 min   Servings: 4

Ingredients

- 3 tbsp olive oil
- 1 minced garlic clove
- 2 tomatoes, sliced
- 1 tbsp soybean paste
- 1 tbsp sesame butter
- 1 cup vegetable cheese, diced
- ½ cup walnuts
- 4 tbsp polenta
- Parsley to taste

- *10 cups of water*
- *10 ½ oz integral spaghetti*
- *Basil*

Instructions

- Heat oil in a skillet and sauté the garlic for 2 minutes.
- Stir in the tomatoes, soybean paste, sesame butter, and vegetable cheese.
- Cook the tomato mixture for 10 minutes.
- Add the walnuts and polenta and stir to mix.
- Add parsley and water to the saucepan and stir.
- Stir the spaghetti into the walnut mixture and cook for 10 minutes.
- Top with the basil to taste and serve.

Nutrition-Per Serving: Calories: 417Kcal, Total Fat: 30g, Total Carbs: 25g, Protein: 14g

Tips: This is a perfect dinner for a busy day. Simple pantry ingredients are required to put this delicious meal on the table in just 20 minutes.

Pork and Peppers (Selsko Meso)

Prep time: 10 min   Cook time: 15 min   Servings: 6

Ingredients

- 1 tbsp vegetable oil
- 1 ½ lb. lean pork loin
- 1 finely chopped onion
- 2 coarsely chopped green pepper
- 2 coarsely chopped tomatoes
- 4 oz chopped mushrooms
- 1 tbsp Vegeta seasoning powder
- ½ cup of water
- 1 tbsp sweet paprika

Instructions

- Heat oil in a skillet over medium heat.
- Sauté the pork for about 3 minutes until it is no longer pink.

- Stir in the onion, green pepper, tomatoes, and mushroom then sauté them for about 5 minutes until the tomatoes exuded their juices.
- Stir in the Vegeta seasoning powder, water, and paprika to the pork.
- Cook the pork for about 5-10 minutes stirring often during the cooking.
- Serve and enjoy.

Nutrition - per serving: Calories: 212 kcal, Total fat: 11g, Carbs: 7g, Protein: 20g

Tips: You had a busy day and are wondering what to put on the table in a few minutes? Selsko Meso consists of pork chops that are perfectly flavored to make an exquisite dish that will satisfy your family for dinner. If you have some other leftover meat or vegetables at home, do not hesitate to add them to this dish.

Cevapcici

Prep time: 2h 30 min   Cook time: 10 min   Servings: 6

Ingredients

- 1 pound ground veal
- ½ pound ground pork
- ½ pound ground lamb (or beef)
- 2 cloves minced clove garlic
- 1 tsp of salt
- Freshly ground black pepper
- 1 tsp of minced hot peppers
- 2 tsp of Kajmak
- 2 tsp of sparkling water (or beef broth)

Instructions

- In a large bowl, mix together all the ingredients.

- Knead well, at least 10 minutes so that the ingredients are well mixed.
- Cover and put into the fridge to rest for at least 2 h (or overnight).
- Once rested, roll the meat mixture into a long, ¾-inch cylinder to make sausage shaped cevapcici. Cut it to a length of 4 inches each roll or as desired.
- Bake cevapcici over the grill (medium heat) for approx. 7 minutes, depending on the thickness and length. Turn a few times during baking to grill all sides evenly.
- Once ready, remove from the grill and serve warm with some flatbread, sliced onion, Kajmak and Ajvar aside.

Nutrition – per serving: Calories: 870kcal, Total Fat: 67g, Carbs: 1g, Protein: 60g

Tips: If you're wondering why we included water in the recipe, it's to keep the cevapcici from sticking to the grill while baking. Pljeskavica, like cevapcici, is prepared in the same manner. Typically, 1 finely chopped onion is added to the mixture, and instead of making rolls, a patty is formed.

Serbian Stuffed Cabbage (Sarma)

| Prep time: 40 min | Cook time: 3 hours | Servings: 6 |

Ingredients

- *1 head cabbage*
- *2 onions*
- *4 tbsp oil*
- *3 garlic cloves*
- *1 cup rice, rinsed*
- *1 pound ground chuck*
- *½ pound ground pork*
- *1 (32-ounce) jar sauerkraut, rinsed and drained*
- *6 medium cured smoked ribs or some other cured smoked meat*
- *3 bay leaves*
- *1 tbsp all-purpose white flour*

- *1 cup beef stock*
- *2 tbsp tomato paste*
- *1 tbsp ground paprika*
- *Salt and black pepper to taste*

Instructions

- Steam the cabbage head until the outer leaves are limp. Let it cool slightly. Separate the leaves.
- Remove the hard ribs from the leaves with a paring knife without breaking them. Save the tougher outer leaves for later, but don't use them for rolling.
- Chop the onions and place it in a nonstick pan with 2 tbsp of oil. Cook over medium heat and stir occasionally. After few minutes, add the rice and chopped garlic. Stir occasionally for another few minutes until the rice gets a glassy texture. Then set aside to cool down a little.
- Combine the ground chuck, ground pork, rice and onion from the pan in a medium mixing bowl. Add some ground paprika, salt and pepper to taste. A tablespoon of water will make it easier to mix.
- On steamed, prepared cabbage leaf place 2 tbsp of filling. Fold the bottom part of the leaf over the filling. Continue with folding the sides to encase the filling. Roll up away from yourself. Use a toothpick to hold it in place if necessary.
- Repeat until the mixture is gone.
- Chop the remaining cabbage, discard the core. Place it on the bottom of the casserole and cover with drained sauerkraut.
- Place the rolls in the casserole seam-side down.
- Cut smoked meat into pieces and space them between the cabbage rolls. Add the bay leaves as well.
- Cover the rolls with reserved tougher cabbage leaves.

- Heat some oil in the saucepan on medium high heat and add flour. Stir until the flour is straw colored. Add beef stock, tomato paste and ground paprika.
- Carefully pour the liquid over the rolls. Then add just enough water over the rolls to not overtop them.
- Cover with a lid and bake for 1hr on 350 F and another 2hr on 325 F in the oven. An alternative way is to simmer for 3hr on the stove.
- Let it rest for 15 minutes before serving. If desired, serve with some bread.

Nutrition-Per Serving: Calories: 651Kcal, Total Fat: 34,9g, Total Carbs: 45,3g, Protein: 39,3g

Tips: Originally, the rolls are made from fermented cabbage leaves, but because they are difficult to find in stores, we can substitute steamed raw cabbage leaves. This dish is typically made in larger quantities and it is consumed 2 -3 days in a row. Sarma can also be frozen for future use.

Serbian Pea Stew with Chicken

| Prep time: 10 min | Cook time: 35 min | Servings: 4 |

Ingredients

- *2 tbsp oil*
- *1 chopped onion*
- *1 chopped carrot*
- *2 chicken thighs, chopped*
- *3 cups of water*
- *1 ½ cup fresh peas*
- *1 tbsp Vegeta*
- *Salt and black pepper to taste*

For the roux

- *4 tbsp oil*
- *1 minced garlic clove*
- *2 tbsp flour*
- *1 tbsp paprika*

Instructions

- Heat oil in a saucepan over medium heat and sauté the onions for 5 minutes.
- Stir in carrots to the onion and sauté them for 5 minutes.
- Add the chicken and 3 cups of water to the carrots and stir to mix. Cook for 5 minutes.
- Stir in the peas, Vegeta, salt, and pepper to the chicken and cook for 7 minutes.
- Reduce the heat to low and simmer for 7 minutes.
- Prepare the roux by heating oil in a skillet.
- Sauté the garlic for 3 minutes, then add flour and cook for further 4 minutes.
- Stir in the paprika and remove the roux from heat.
- Pour the roux into the stew and stir. Cook for another 3 min.
- Serve while hot. You can garnish the stew with herbs of your choice!

Nutrition-Per Serving: Calories: 436Kcal, Total Fat: 37g, Total Carbs: 10g, Protein: 17g

Tips: Do you have excess peas from your garden? Prepare this yummy dish for your family dinner on the weekend. It is simple to put up together yet comes out yummy.

Potato Stuffed Peppers

| Prep time: 25 min | Cook time: 1 h 15 min | Servings: 6 |

Ingredients

- 1 cup olive oil
- ½ onion, finely chopped
- 2 celery ribs, finely chopped
- 2 carrots, peeled and shredded
- 5 garlic cloves, chopped
- Salt to taste
- ¼ tbsp black pepper
- 5 potatoes, peeled and shredded
- 2 tbsp chopped parsley
- ¼ cup water

- *6 red bell peppers*
- *2 zucchinis, peeled and shredded*
- *1 cup Ajvar*
- *Parsley for garnish*

Instructions

- Heat oil in a skillet over medium heat and sauté onions for 8 minutes.
- Stir in celery and carrots and cook for 5 minutes.
- Stir garlic, salt, pepper, potatoes, parsley, and water into the skillet and cook for 10 minutes.
- Clean the peppers and cut off the tops. Discard the pepper tops.
- Remove seeds from the bell pepper and sprinkle them with salt.
- Add the zucchini to the potatoes and mix.
- Fill the peppers with the potato filling and place them on a baking sheet that has been mist with cooking spray.
- Preheat the oven to 350° F.
- Bake the stuffed peppers for 1 hour.
- Serve with Ajvar and top with parsley.

Nutrition-Per Serving: Calories: 480Kcal, Total Fat: 39g, Total Carbs: 20g, Protein: 15g

Tips: Another version of stuffed vegetables, that locals love. Stuffed peppers are a fancy way of serving veggies in your meal. They are hearty, filling and even your kids will love them. You can play with the filling, depending on your taste: try out cheese, minced meat, veggies with bread crumbs, Saur cream, or other desired mixtures.

Chicken with Peppers and Mushroom

| Prep time: 15 min | Cook time: 40 min | Servings: 3 |

Ingredients

- Paprika to taste
- Salt and black pepper to taste
- 3 chicken breasts, cut into small pieces
- 2 tbsp oil
- 2 red bell peppers, seed removed and diced
- 2 green bell peppers, seed removed and diced
- 1 onion, chopped
- 2 minced garlic cloves
- 1 chili peppers, finely chopped

- *1 mushroom, chopped*
- *2 tbsp tomato paste*
- *1 cup dry white wine*

Instructions

- In a bowl mix paprika, salt, and black pepper.
- Rub the chicken legs with the seasoning mixture.
- Heat oil in a saucepan on a stovetop and sauté the bell peppers, onions, garlic, and chili peppers for 5 minutes.
- Stir in the mushrooms and tomato paste to the vegetables and cook for 5 minutes.
- Transfer the vegetables to a baking tray and place the chicken pieces on top.
- Pour wine over the chicken and cook for 30 minutes.
- Serve and enjoy.

Nutrition-Per Serving: Calories: 512Kcal, Total Fat: 20g, Total Carbs: 25g, Protein: 56g

Tips: This chicken and mushroom make a great accompaniment to rice or mashed potatoes. Even better, it uses ingredients readily available in your pantry.

Herb and Garlic Roasted Leg of Lamb

| Prep time: 10 min | Cook time: 2 h | Servings: 6 |

Ingredients

- *5 lb. leg of lamb*
- *3 garlic cloves, minced*
- *2 tbsp rosemary*
- *1 tbsp thyme*
- *1 tbsp salt*
- *¼ tbsp black pepper*
- *3 tbsp lemon juice*
- *Rosemary for garnishing*

Instructions

- Preheat the oven to 325° F.
- Dry the lamb with a paper towel and make several ½ -inch cuts on the lamb.
- Place the minced garlic into the cuts.
- In a bowl mix the rosemary, thyme, salt, and pepper.
- Rub the lamb with lemon juice and then with the seasoning mixture.
- Place the lamb on a roasting pan and roast for 2 hours.
- Garnish the lamb with rosemary and serve.

Nutrition-Per Serving: Calories: 485Kcal, Total Fat: 46g, Total Carbs: 17g, Protein: 7g

Tips: Lamb is one of the favorite types of meat in Serbia. This is a tender and hearty lamb leg that is effortless to prepare but very tasty. Serve with your favorite salad or dip.

Filled Yellow Peppers (Punjena Paprika)

Prep time: 15 min   Cook time: 2h 30 min   Servings: 4

Ingredients

- *8 medium sized, round yellow peppers*
- *1 lb. minced pork*
- *1 lb. minced beef*
- *2 garlic cloves (minced)*
- *1 egg*
- *1 tbsp of pork fat (or butter)*
- *1 onion, chopped*
- *1 tbsp sweet red paprika*

- *1.5 handfuls of white rice*
- *Salt and black pepper to taste*

For the gravy

- *1 tbsp of sweet red paprika*
- *3-4 tbsp all-purpose white flour*
- *1 tsp of sugar*
- *1 tbsp of pork fat (or butter)*
- *1 can of tomato sauce*
- *Salt and black pepper to taste*
- *Some water*
- *2 bay leaves*

Instructions

- Wash the peppers, then gently remove the cover with the stem and seeds. Discard the seeds, but keep the covers for later use.
- In a large bowl, add the meat, garlic and egg. Season to taste with salt and pepper and mix until well combined.
- In a pan over medium heat, melt the pork fat (or butter) and fry the onion until it becomes yellow. Add it to the meat mixture.
- In line with the manufacturer's instructions, cook the rice halfway before adding it to the meat. Mix well with the meat mixture.
- Fill the peppers halfway up, then put the reserved covers with the stem on. Set aside.
- Add 1-2 cups of water to a large pot and bring to a boil.
- Meanwhile, prepare the gravy in a separate pan: In a pot, melt the fat (or butter) over medium heat and add the sugar, flour, paprika and tomato sauce. Stir well.
- Add some water if the gravy is too thick. Add salt and pepper to taste, and 2 bay leaves. Stir well.

- Pour the sauce into the hot water and mix well to get a homogeneous sauce. It should not be too watery.
- Add paprikas to the gravy, tops up, tightly next to each other. If necessary, add more water – paprikas should be covered with liquid.
- Cook over medium heat for approx. 2 hours, season with additional salt and pepper if necessary. Once cooked, remove the bay leaves and leave to rest for 30 minutes.
- Serve with some mashed potatoes or bread and enjoy!

Nutrition-Per Serving: Calories: 258Kcal, Total Fat: 12,1g, Total Carbs: 24g, Protein: 14,5g

Tips: For a fuller and more consistent taste, leave paprikas to cool completely, then reheat them before consuming. Some individuals add cinnamon or a little bit of red wine rather than water to their gravy. Basically, every family has a slightly different recipe. This dish is usually made in large quantities - extra portions are frozen for future use.

SOUPS AND STEWS

Beef Broth

| Prep time: 30 min | Cook time: 7 h | Servings: 4 |

Ingredients

- 4 lb. beef bones
- 2 onions
- 2 carrots
- 2 celery sticks
- 2 tomatoes
- 4 ½ liter cold water
- 1 handful parsley
- 1 tbsp thyme
- Salt and pepper

Instructions

- Heat your oven to 450F.
- Bake meat in the oven for 30 minutes. Add onions, carrots, celery and tomatoes to the baking pan.
- Bake for an additional 30 minutes. Transfer everything to a pot and add water
- Bring the soup to a boil. Remove the foam on the surface with a spoon.
- Add parsley, thyme, salt and pepper to the pot and cook for 6 hours. Cook the soup ensuring the bones are covered by water.
- Strain the soup and remove as much fat as you can. Let it cool down and place it in the fridge.
- Remove the fat layer on top and serve the broth.

Nutrition- Per Serving: Calories 143kcal, Total Fat: 5g, Carbs: 11g, Protein: 25g

Tips: This is a nutritious and delicious beef broth that can be served for lunch or strained ingredients served as a side dish.

Pork and Pepper Stew (Leskovacka Muckalica)

Prep time: 20 min   Cook time: 1h 45 min   Servings: 6

Ingredients

- 4 tbsp butter
- 4 tbsp olive oil
- 2 lb. pork tenderloin, sliced into strips ½ -inch thick
- 3 onions, cut into rings
- 2 tbsp flour
- 3 tbsp hot paprika powder
- 1 green pepper, seed removed and cut into strips
- 1 red pepper, seed removed and cut into strips
- 1 yellow pepper, seed removed and cut into strips
- 3 fresh serrano peppers, cut into rings

- *1 cup beef stock*
- *3 tbsp tomato paste*
- *3 minced garlic cloves*
- *1 tbsp salt*
- *1 bay leaf*
- *Chopped parsley for topping*

Instructions

- Heat 2 tbsp of butter and 2 tbsp of oil in a skillet over medium heat. Brown both sides of the pork for 5 minutes.
- Remove the pork from the skillet using a slotted spoon and set aside.
- Add the remaining butter and oil to the skillet and sauté the onions for 2 minutes.
- Stir in flour and paprika to the onions and cook for 2 minutes while stirring often.
- Add pork, peppers, beef stock, tomato paste, garlic, salt, and bay leaf to the skillet and mix well.
- Bring the pork stew to a boil then reduce the heat to low.
- Cook the pork for 1 ½ hour.
- Top the pork stew with parsley and serve.

Nutrition-Per Serving: Calories: 407Kcal, Total Fat: 23g, Total Carbs: 8g, Protein: 42g

Tips: Make this hearty pork and pepper stew your family's favorite weeknight dinner. The veggies make the stew bright and colorful while packing it with nutrients.

Serbian Lentils

| Prep time: 20 min | Cook time: 5 h 30 min | Servings: 2 |

Ingredients

- *1 ¾ oz lentils*
- *3 tbsp sunflower oil*
- *4 onions, chopped*
- *2 minced garlic cloves*
- *1 eggplant, peeled and chopped*
- *1 carrot, chopped*
- *2 tomatoes, diced*
- *Salt to taste*
- *Parsley*

Instructions

- Soak the lentils in water for 5 hours.
- Rinse the lentils and drain the excess water.
- Heat oil in a saucepan and sauté the onions for 2 minutes.
- Add the garlic and sauté for 2 minutes.
- Stir in the lentils, eggplant, carrot, and tomatoes to the saucepan.
- Season the lentils with salt and simmer for 30 minutes.
- Top with parsley and serve.

Nutrition-Per Serving: Calories: 395Kcal, Total Fat: 22g, Total Carbs: 48g, Protein: 9g

Tips: This is a comforting dish for a cold evening. The lentils in the dish help stay satiated until the next meal.

Freshwater Fish Stew

| Prep time: 15 min | Cook time: 45 min | Servings: 4 |

Ingredients

- 4 tbsp vegetable oil
- 4 cups onions, chopped
- 3 minced garlic cloves
- 1 tbsp salt
- 1 tbsp sweet paprika powder
- ⅓ tbsp hot paprika powder
- 4 peppercorns
- 6 ½ cup water
- 2 lb. freshwater fish, cut into small pieces
- 1 cup white wine
- Parsley

Instructions

- Pour oil into a skillet and heat it over medium heat.
- Sauté the onions for 2 minutes.
- Add the garlic, salt, paprika, and peppercorns to the skillet.
- Add ½ cup of water to the garlic mixture and bring it to a boil.
- Mash the garlic mixture using a potato masher.
- Add the remaining water to the mashed garlic mixture and bring it to a boil.
- Stir the fish and white wine into the soup and cook for 30 minutes.
- Top the fish stew with parsley and serve.

Nutrition-Per Serving: Calories: 485Kcal, Total Fat: 46g, Total Carbs: 17g, Protein: 7g

Tips: This fish stew perfectly fits your dietary needs. It is not only healthy and flavorful but also simple to prepare.

Chicken Stew (Pileci Paprikas)

| Prep time: 10 min | Cook time: 1 h 10 min | Servings: 10 |

Ingredients

- ½ cup olive oil
- 1 onion, chopped
- 6 potatoes, peeled and chopped
- 1 whole chicken cut into pieces
- 1 tbsp salt
- 1 tbsp Vegeta
- 1 tbsp ground red pepper
- ½ cup of water
- Toppings: chopped red peppers and parsley

For the dumplings:

- *1 cup wheat flour*
- *1 egg*
- *½ tbsp salt*
- *½ cup of water*

Instructions

- Pour oil into a saucepan and heat it over medium heat.
- Sauté the onion for 2 minutes. Add the potatoes to the saucepan and stir.
- Place the chicken pieces over the potatoes and add salt, Vegeta, red pepper, and water. Cook the chicken for 45 minutes.
- Meanwhile, in a bowl prepare the dumpling by mixing flour, egg, salt, and water until ductile dough is formed.
- Make small dumplings from the dough.
- Using a tablespoon, drop the dumplings in the cooking stew piece by piece.
- Cook the stew for 15 minutes.
- Top the chicken stew with red pepper and parsley.
- Serve and enjoy.

Nutrition-Per Serving: Calories: 544Kcal, Total Fat: 18g, Total Carbs: 62g, Protein: 33g

Tips: This an aromatic and flavorful meal to prepare for a great weeknight meal. Serve the chicken with warm rice or pasta.

Cold Cucumber Soup

| Prep time: 15 min | Cook time: 0 min | Servings: 2 |

Ingredients

- *2 peeled cucumbers, freshly chopped*
- *7 dl yoghurt*
- *1 ¼ cup milk*
- *1 tbsp onions, chopped*
- *Salt and pepper to taste*
- *3 tbsp parsley*

Instructions

- Mix all ingredients until well mixed (you can use a mixer).

- Place in the fridge and let cool.
- Stir the soup and pour into soup bowls.
- Garnish with parsley leaves and enjoy.

Nutrition- Per Serving: Calories 161kcal, Total Fat: 7g, Carbs: 17g, Protein: 11g

Tips: This is toothsome soup perfect for the hot summer. It's very easy to make yet packed with nutrients and it's very filling.

Tomato Soup

| Prep time: 15 min | Cook time: 30 min | Servings: 2 |

Ingredients

- 1 tbsp flour
- 1 tbsp oil
- 2 lb tomato juice
- 1 tbsp sugar
- 2 basil leaves
- Salt and pepper
- 3 tbsp butter

Instructions

- Fry flour in oil then add tomato juice.
- When the tomato juice is well cooked add sugar, basil, salt, and pepper and cook for 15 minutes.
- Serve the soup with butter and rice or pasta. Enjoy.

Nutrition- Per Serving: Calories 327kcal, Total Fat: 24g, Carbs: 28g, Protein: 4g

Tips: Is it tomato season and you are looking for different ways to use tomatoes? Here is a tasty recipe for you.

Cauliflower Corba

| Prep time: 10 min | Cook time: 30 min | Servings: 8 |

Ingredients

- *2 tbsp oil*
- *1 onion, chopped*
- *1 carrot, thinly sliced*
- *1 celery stalk*
- *1 tomato, chopped*
- *1 potato, diced*
- *1 head cauliflower, chopped*
- *1 tbsp dried thyme*
- *1 quart vegetable broth*
- *¼ tbsp black pepper*

- *salt to taste*
- *2 tbsp flour*

Instructions

- Heat 1 tbsp of oil in a soup pot over medium heat.
- Sauté onions until golden brown. Add carrots and celery and fry for 2 minutes.
- Add tomatoes, potatoes, cauliflower, thyme and black pepper to the pot. Cook for an additional1 minute.
- Add broth and bring to a boil. If the vegetables are not well covered, add 1 cup of water.
- Simmer until the vegetables are tender. Add salt to taste.
- Heat 1 tbsp of oil on a saucepan and add flour. Stir well then add a ladle of broth. Stir until smooth.
- Add the roux to the soup in the pot and cook for 10 minutes.
- Adjust seasoning and serve.

Nutrition- Per Serving: Calories 371kcal, Total Fat: 17g, Carbs: 41g, Protein: 16g

Tips: A big bowl of Serbian cauliflower soup is all you need on those chilly rainy days. It's easy to put together and the thickness of the soup without cream takes cauliflower soup to the next level.

Lamb and Cabbage Soup (Ličani)

| Prep time: 15 min | Cook time: 30 min | Servings: 5 |

Ingredients

- *2 lb. BBQ lamb*
- *4 quarts water*
- *5 carrots, sliced*
- *1 cabbage head chopped*
- *¾ cup rice*
- *¼ cup ketchup*
- *1 jalapeno pepper, slit*
- *2 tbsp vegetable base*
- *Garlic salt*
- *Salt and pepper to taste*
- *¼ bag fin noodles*

Instructions

- Add meat and water to a soup pot and bring to a boil. Simmer then remove meat from the bones.
- Return meat to the pot. Add all the ingredients except noodles and cook until the carrots are well cooked.
- Add noodles and cook for an additional 5 minutes. Serve the soup warm, aside with some bread.

Nutrition- Per Serving: Calories 178kcal, Total Fat: 12g, Carbs: 31g, Protein: 5g

Tips: This Serbian lamb and cabbage soup comes out just perfect. The ketchup enhances the amazing combination of lamb and cabbage.

Clear Fish Soup

| Prep time: 15 min | Cook time: 30 min | Servings: 4 |

Ingredients

- 2 lb. mixed fish
- 3 carrots
- 1 onion, sliced
- 1 celery sticks
- 2 garlic cloves
- 5 peppercorns
- Chopped parsley
- Salt to taste
- 1 spoon olive oil
- 1 cup rice

Instructions

- Scale and gut all the fish. Add them to a soup pot. Add fresh water until well covered.
- Add carrots, onions, celery, garlic, peppercorns, parsley, and salt. Simmer for 30 minutes. Remove the fish from the soup and remove all bones.
- Strain the soup, add oil, and rice then return the fish pieces back.
- Serve the soup with crusty bread. Enjoy.

Nutrition- Per Serving: Calories 533kcal, Total Fat: 18g, Carbs: 71g, Protein: 21g

Tips: If you have plenty of different fish, or are a seafood lover, then this is a recipe you must try. It is very easy to put together yet comes out so tasty that you will make it all the time.

Beans Stew (Pasulj)

| Prep time: 10 min | Cook time: 2 h 20 min | Servings: 4 |

Ingredients

- 1 can of white beans
- 1 l water
- 1 cup of beef broth
- 2 medium onions (chopped)
- 4 garlic cloves (minced)
- 400 g smoked bacon (or raw bacon), sliced into pieces
- 2 laurel leaves
- 1 tbsp of pork fat
- 1 tbsp of flour
- 1 tsp of sweet paprika
- 1 carrot (chopped)
- 15 oz. can tomato sauce
- 1 Parsley root (chopped)

- *Salt and pepper to taste*

Instructions

- If you are using fresh beans, wash and soak them overnight. If the beans are canned, they are ready to go right away.
- Add the beans to cold water, over medium heat. Cook for about 15 minutes, until the beans soften. Set aside.
- To a separate pan, melt the pork fat over medium heat. Add the flour and stir quickly, 1 or 2 mint, until it smells good.
- Add the onions, parsley root, carrot, bacon, garlic, laurel leaves and paprika and stir for 5 minutes, until the ingredients brown a little. Add tomato sauce and stir.
- Add water and the beans, beef broth and pepper to the pan and cook over medium heat for about 2 hours (or until the beans are completely softened).
- Salt to taste when the beans are already cooked.
- Cut the bacon into pieces and serve Pasulj in bowls – add a few pieces of meat to every bowl.

Nutrition-Per Serving: Calories: 503Kcal, Total Fat: 104g, Total Carbs: 76g, Protein: 28g

Tips: The combination of Pork and beans serves a delicious yet filling meal for your family or friends coming over for dinner. Usually, locals serve Pasulj with a few slices of fresh bread aside.

SALADS

Serbian Coleslaw

| Prep time: 20 min | Cook time: 0 min | Servings: 5 |

Ingredients

- 1 lb. cabbage, shredded
- ¼ cup carrots, shredded
- ¼ cups onion, chopped
- 3 tbsp parsley, chopped
- ½ cup olive oil
- 1 tbsp sugar
- ⅛ tbsp celery seed
- 1 tbsp vinegar
- ⅛ tbsp salt
- ½ tbsp white pepper
- 1 tbsp lemon juice

Instructions

- In a mixing bowl, mix cabbage, carrots, onions, and parsley.
- In another mixing, mix oil, sugar, celery seed, vinegar, salt, pepper and lemon juice.
- Toss the oil mixture with the cabbage mixture until well coated.
- Cover and refrigerate for at least 3 hours or overnight.
- Mix well and adjust the seasoning.

Nutrition- Per Serving: Calories 29kcal, Total Fat: 0g, Carbs: 7g, Protein: 1g

Tips: This is a perfect salad to serve during warm weather. The recipe uses vinegar and oil instead of mayo or heavy cream and is therefore healthy, low in calories and refreshing.

Šopska Salata

Prep time: 10 min Cook time: 0 min Servings: 4

Ingredients

- *1 cucumber, sliced*
- *2 tomatoes, diced*
- *1 bell pepper, sliced*
- *2 scallions, sliced*
- *2 tbsp sunflower oil*
- *2 tbsp white wine vinegar*
- *Salt and pepper to taste*
- *8 tbsp Serbian white cheese (or feta cheese)*
- *Chives for garnish*

Instructions

- Add all the vegetables to a salad bowl.
- In a small mixing bowl, whisk oil, vinegar, salt, and pepper until well mixed.
- Toss the vegetable with the dressing until well coated.
- Top the salad with cheese and garnish with chives. Enjoy.

Nutrition- Per Serving: Calories: 188kcal, Total Fat: 15g, Carbs: 9g, Protein: 6g

Tips: Šopska Salata is a simple yet light and refreshing salad that everyone will love. It is very popular among the locals and is usually served next to grilled meat. It can be stored in the refrigerator for several days.

Oil and Vinegar Potato Salad

Prep time: 10 min   Cook time: 30 min   Servings: 4

Ingredients

- 2 lb. Yukon gold potatoes
- ¼ red onions, finely sliced
- ¼ cup red wine vinegar
- ½ tbsp sugar
- ¼ cup virgin olive oil
- 1 tbsp salt
- Freshly ground black pepper

Instructions

- Bring water in a pot to a boil.
- Meanwhile, peel and slice the potatoes into 1-inch slices. Add the potatoes into the boiling water.
- Cook the potatoes for 10-15 minutes or until they can easily be poked using a fork.
- Drain water to a separate bowl and save for later. Let the potatoes sit in the fridge for a few minutes to cool.
- Add the potatoes and onions to a mixing bowl, then add wine vinegar, sugar and a few tbsp of leftover water from the potatoes. Let marinate.
- Pour oil over the mixture and season with salt and pepper to taste.
- Stir until well mixed. If too dry, add some more leftover potato water to the mix. The salad should be silky and moist.
- If desired, you can garnish the salad with a bit of parsley or other herbs by choice.

Nutrition- Per Serving: Calories 338kcal, Total Fat: 14g, Carbs: 49g, Protein: 6g

Tips: This is a delicious and super easy to make potato salad that you will love. You can use some leftover boiled potatoes to make this salad. Prepare the salad a few hours before serving to allow the juices to fully absorb into the potatoes. It's perfect for summer or outdoor parties and makes a great side dish to any type of meat.

Garlic Roasted Peppers (Belolučena Paprika)

Prep time: 10 min Cook time: 2 h Servings: 4

Ingredients

- *8 roasted peppers, peeled*
- *6 garlic cloves*
- *½ cup white vinegar*
- *5 tbsp sunflower oil*
- *1 tbsp fresh parsley, chopped*
- *½ tbsp salt*

Instructions

- In a mixing bowl, mix garlic, vinegar, oil, parsley and salt until well combined.

- Spoon 1 tbsp of the mixture on the chilling dish. Arrange the peppers on the dish without overlapping them.
- Spoon 2 tbsp of the mixture on the peppers and layer another layer of peppers in the opposite direction.
- Repeat the process while layering the peppers in an alternative direction until all peppers and the mixture is used.
- Chill in the fridge for at least 2 hours. Enjoy.

Nutrition- Per Serving: Calories 206kcal, Total Fat: 18g, Carbs: 11g, Protein: 2g

Tips: This is one of the most recognized salad dishes in Serbia. If you really love garlic, this might become your new family favorite. Experience the freshness of peppers even when they aren't in season. You can store this dish in the refrigerator for 2-3 days.

Cucumber Salad with Sour Cream

| Prep time: 20 min | Cook time:20 min | Servings: 4 |

Ingredients

- 4 cucumbers, sliced
- 2 Garlic cloves, grated
- 3 tbsp sour cream (or yoghurt)
- Salt and pepper to taste
- Fresh dill or parsley for garnish

Instructions

- Add cucumbers to a mixing bowl and sprinkle with salt.

- Set aside for 10-15 min, until the water comes out of the cucumbers. Drain.
- Add sour cream or yoghurt. Adjust pepper and salt to taste.
- Garnish with dill or parsley.
- Serve and enjoy.

Nutrition- Per Serving: Calories 67kcal, Total Fat: 2g, Carbs: 12g, Protein: 2g

Tips: If you are looking for a perfect salad to go along with BBQs, then this is the salad for you. It is packed with nutrients yet very easy to prepare. If desired, do not hesitate to add some finely sliced onions to the mix.

Red Beet and Carrot Salad

Prep time: 10 min Cook time: 0 min Servings: 6

Ingredients

- ½ lb. carrot, grated
- ½ lb. red beet, grated
- 2 garlic cloves, chopped
- Fresh mint leaves
- 2 tbsp oil
  3 tbsp Plums Vinegar
- Salt and pepper to taste

Instructions

- Add carrots and beets in a mixing bowl and mix well.

- Add garlic and mint leaves and stir again.
- Add oil, vinegar, salt and pepper.
- Serve sprinkled with fresh mint.

Nutrition- Per Serving: Calories 174kcal, Total Fat: 5g, Carbs: 8g, Protein: 1g

Tips: This is one of my favorite salads. It's made with shredded beet and carrot with oil and vinegar dressing instead of creamy dressing. It is quick, easy to put together and very delicious.

DESSERTS

Chocolate Balls (Čokoladne Kuglice)

| Prep time: 15 min | Cook time: 0 min | Servings: 12 |

Ingredients

- 2 cups almond, grind
- 1 cup chocolate
- ½ cup powdered sugar
- 2 egg yolks
- 1 shot rum
- 1 cup Cocoa flour
- ½ cup Cocoa

Instructions

- Add chocolate, sugar, egg and rum into a mixing bowl.

- Mix until smooth.
- Form balls using the dough and roll them in the cocoa flour.
- Serve or keep in an airtight container for several days.

Nutrition- Per Serving: Calories 203kcal, Total Fat: 13g, Carbs: 19g, Protein: 6g

Tips: These are delicious chocolate balls that do not require cooking. Serve them after dinner to friends coming over or during parties.

Walnut Nutmeg Cookie

| Prep time: 10 min | Cook time: 15 min | Servings: 20 pieces |

Ingredients

- *1 package cookie mix*
- *1 tbsp cinnamon*
- *1 ½ tbsp nutmeg*
- *½ tbsp cloves*
- *½ cup chocolate chips*
- *½ cup chopped walnuts*

Instructions

- Preheat your oven 350°F and line 2 cookie sheets with foil.
- Add the cookie mix to a mixing bowl. Add the spices and wet ingredients as per the instructions on the package. Mix until well combined
- Add chocolate chips and walnuts and mix until well incorporated.

- Scoop the dough onto the cookie sheet and flatten using the back of the spoon. Bake for 10 minutes or until firm.
- Swerve when warm.

Nutrition- Per Serving: Calories 531kcal, Total Fat: 5g, Carbs: 8g, Protein: 7g

Tips: These are effortless cookies that everyone in your family or friends coming over will love. You may use more ingredients of choice to make these cookies as impressive as possible.

Serbian Fast Pastries

Prep time: 15 min   Cook time: 30 min   Servings: 6

Ingredients

- *2 eggs*
- *1 cup white coffee milk*
- *1 ½ cup sugar*
- *1 cup semolina*
- *1 cup nuts, ground*
- *½ cup oil*
- *2 apples, grated*
- *3 tbsp baking powder*
- *2 tbsp flour*
- *¼ cup raisins*

Glaze

- ½ cup chocolate
- 2 tbsp sugar
- 4 tbsp water
- 2 drops oil

Instructions

- Add all the ingredients to a mixing bowl and mix until well combined. Pour the mixture into a baking dish.
- Bake in the oven at the highest heat for 20 minutes.
- Meanwhile, mix the glaze ingredients in a saucepan and bring it to a boil.
- Pour over the pastries and serve.
- You can portion with a spoon.

Nutrition- Per Serving: Calories 301kcal, Total Fat: 15g, Carbs: 42g, Protein: 6g

Tips: This is a pretty fast and yummy dessert that may become your kid's new favorite.

Tulumbe

Prep time: 30 min | Cook time: 20 min | Servings: 12

Ingredients

For the Syrup

- *6 ¼ cups sugar*
- *4 cups water*
- *1 tbsp vanilla*
- *1 tbsp lemon juice*

For the Dough

- *6 oz unsalted butter*
- *1 ½ cup of water*

- *½ tbsp salt*
- *1 ½ cups all-purpose flour*
- *6 eggs, beaten*

Directions

- Add the syrup ingredients to a saucepan and bring them to a boil over medium heat.
- Cook the syrup over low heat for 15 minutes.
- Pour the syrup into 2 bowls and allow it to cool completely.
- Meanwhile, preheat the oven to 425°F and line the baking sheet with parchment paper.
- Melt butter in a saucepan then add water and mix.
- Add salt and flour to the saucepan and mix until dough is formed.
- Mix the eggs with the dough to form smooth dough.
- Put the dough in a pastry bag and make shapes 5cm long.
- Place the shaped dough pieces on the baking sheet and bake them for 20 minutes.
- Remove the Tulumbe from the oven and soak them in the syrup overnight before serving.

Nutrition - per serving: Calories: 571kcal, Total fat: 14g, Carbs: 110g, Protein: 3g

Tips: This is an incredibly delicious and sweet dessert for sweet teeth. The syrup used to soak the pastry gives the Tulumbe a fresh, slightly citrusy, and sweet flavor.

White Bayadere (Bela Bajadera)

Prep time: 10 min   Cook time: 30 min   Servings: 12

Ingredients

- ½ cup crystal sugar
- ¼ cup water
- 1 cup biscuits, ground
- ½ cup butter
- 2 molten chocolate bars

Filling

- ½ cup powdered sugar
- ¼ cup water
- ¾ cup powdered milk
- ¼ cup butter

Instructions

- Add sugar, water and butter to a saucepan and heat until sugar dissolves completely.
- Add biscuits to the saucepan and mix to combine.
- Put the mixture on a buttered baking pan and roll it out.
- Set it in the fridge to cool down.
- Pour melted chocolate over the cake and spread it to create a thin chocolate layer. Put it in the fridge until chocolate hardens completely.
- Make the filling. Bring water and sugar to a boil in a saucepan. Combine powdered milk and butter in a mixing bowl and mix well. Add hot sugary water to a mixing bowl and mix well until smooth.
- Spread the filling over the chocolate layer evenly
- Before cutting it into sticks, let it rest in the fridge for at least 2-3 hours

Nutrition- Per Serving: Calories 307kcal, Total Fat: 18g, Carbs: 38g, Protein: 3g

Tips: Just like grownups these cake sticks are loved by children. They are super easy to put together yet leave your taste buds satiated.

Girls' Ring (Devojački Prsten)

Prep time: 15 min   Cook time: 30 min   Servings: 8

Ingredients

- 1 ¼ cup flour
- 4 oz candied fruit, chopped
- 2 tbsp vanilla sugar
- ½ cup powdered sugar
- 4 eggs
- ½ cup butter
- ½ cup raspberry juice
- 8 balls ice cream

Instructions

- In a mixing bowl, mix flour, candied fruit, sugar, egg, and butter until well combined.
- Pour the mixture into 8 greased molds (ring shaped if possible) and bake for 20 minutes at 395°F.
- Put the cakes on a platter and let chill for a few minutes.
- Pour raspberry juice over the cakes to moist them.
- Place an ice cream ball alongside each cake.
- Serve and enjoy!

Nutrition- Per Serving: Calories 295kcal, Total Fat: 14g, Carbs: 37g, Protein: 5g

Tips: Who doesn't love ice cream? The good news is that you can make it right at your home at a pocket friendly price and as much as you want.

Serbian Vanilla Slice (Krempita)

| Prep time: 15 min | Cook time: 30 min | Servings: 25 pieces |

Ingredients

- *4 cups milk*
- *2 tbsp vanilla sugar*
- *8 eggs*
- *2 cups sugar*
- *1 ½ cup flour*
- *1 package puff pastry sheets*

Instructions

- Spread the pastry sheets to form 2 dough sheets that can fit a pan. Make square slashes on the sheets and bake them.
- In a saucepan, bring milk and vanilla sugar to a boil.

- Add egg yolks and ¾ of the sugar in a separate saucepan. Whisk in flour then pour boiled milk.
- Reduce heat and cook the cream until it thickens.
- Mix egg whites and the remaining sugar then add into the cream. Stir the mixture well then add it to the bottom crust.
- Cover it with the top crust and leave it to cool. Cut into slices and sprinkle with powdered sugar.
- Serve and enjoy.

Nutrition- Per Serving: Calories 137kcal, Total Fat: 3g, Carbs: 25g, Protein: 5g

Tips: This Serbian vanilla slice will be a crowd pleaser in your family gathering. It will be a hit and everyone will be talking about it and asking for more.

Walnut Pie (Baklava)

Prep time: 45 min   Cook time: 30 min   Servings: 16 pieces

Ingredients

- 1 lb. walnuts, ground
- 8 oz raisins
- 8 oz sugar
- 1 lb. phyllo pastry sheets
- 4 oz oil
- 16 oz water
- 1 lb. sugar
- 1 lemon, sliced

Instructions

- In a mixing bowl, mix walnuts, raisins and sugar.

- Place 1 pastry sheet in a deep dish and sprinkle with oil. Repeat with two more sheets.
- Spread 5 tbsp of the walnut mixture and layer another phyllo sheet at the top. Sprinkle with oil and repeat until all the walnut mixture is used.
- Place 3 phyllo sheets and sprinkle with oil for the top
- Preheat your oven to 375°F.
- Cut the phyllo into rectangles and bake them for 30 minutes.
- Meanwhile, boil water and add 1 lb. sugar until it gets sticky. Add the lemon slices.
- Pour the sugar mixture over the Suva pita and refrigerate for 24 hours. Cut into pieces and serve.

Nutrition - Per Serving: Calories 411kcal, Total Fat: 27g, Carbs: 39g, Protein: 7g

Tips: This is an addicting dessert that you will love. It's hearty, very easy to make and satisfies all of your sweet cravings. If desired, you can mix in different types of nuts, such as pistachios, hazelnuts or others, according to your taste.

Serbian No Bake Sand Cake

| Prep time: 30 min | Cook time: 0 min | Servings: 8 pieces |

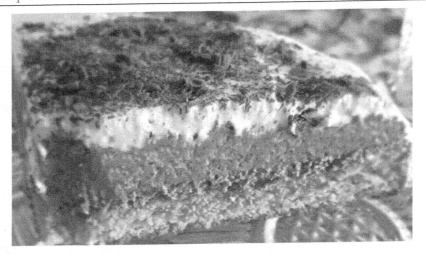

Ingredients

- *3 cups cold milk*
- *12 oz vanilla pudding and pie filling*
- *3 sticks butter, unsalted*
- *2 cups graham cracker crumbs*
- *2 ¼ cup unsweetened coconut, shredded*
- *2 ¼ cups walnuts, ground*

Instructions

- Grease a springform cake pan and set it aside.

Graham cracker Layer

- Pour 1 cup of milk into a mixing bowl.

- Add 4 oz of the pudding mix then whisk until well mixed.
- In another bowl, beat 1 stick of butter with a hand mixer until smooth.
- Add the pudding mix and mix until well combined. Fold in the crumbs then spread the mixture on the pan.

Coconut Layer

- Pour 1 cup of milk in a mixing bowl. Add 4 oz of the pudding mix then whisk until well mixed.
- In another bowl, beat 1 stick of butter with a hand mixer until smooth.
- Add the pudding mix and mix until well combined. Fold in the coconut then spread the mixture over the first layer.

Walnut Layer

- Pour 1 cup of milk in a mixing bowl. Add 4 oz of the pudding mix then whisk until well mixed.
- In another bowl, beat 1 stick of butter with a hand mixer until smooth.
- Add the pudding mix and mix until well combined. Fold in the walnuts then spread the mixture over the coconut layer.
- Top the cake with whipped cream or decorate it as desired.

Nutrition- Per Serving: Calories 261kcal, Total Fat: 18g, Carbs: 22g, Protein: 3g

Tips: Looking for a dessert that will woah your family members during a family gathering? These multi layered cakes taste like a vacation. The best part is it requires no baking and is ready in 30 minutes.

Made in the USA
Middletown, DE
25 January 2022